SPACE

Stars

Robin Birch

MACMILLAN
LIBRARY

First published in 2001 by
MACMILLAN EDUCATION AUSTRALIA PTY LTD
627 Chapel Street, South Yarra 3141

Associated companies and representatives
throughout the world

National Library of Australia
cataloguing in publication data

Birch, Robin.
Stars.

Includes index.
ISBN 0 7329 6561 6.

1. Stars—Juvenile literature. I. Title. (Series: Macmillan young library. Space).

523.8

Edited by Carmel Heron and Louisa Kost
Cover and text design by Anne Stanhope
Illustrations by Frey Micklethwait
Printed in China

Acknowledgements
The author and the publisher are grateful to the following for permission to reproduce copyright material:

Cover photograph: The star cluster Pleiades, courtesy of NASA, supplied by Astrovisuals.
Photographs courtesy of: Astrovisuals, pp. 13, 26; Lochman Transparencies/Dick Beilby, p. 20; NASA, supplied by Astrovisuals, pp. 1, 5, 22, 23, 24, 25, 29; National Optical Australian Observatory, supplied by Astrovisuals, p. 28; PhotoDisc, p. 4; Photo Essentials, p. 19; Photolibrary.com/IT Stock International, p. 27.

While every care has been taken to trace and acknowledge copyright the publishers tender their apologies for any accidental infringement where copyright has proved untraceable.

Contents

Stars

There are millions of stars in the sky. We can see them at night, after the Sun has set. Stars are hot, glowing balls of **gas**.

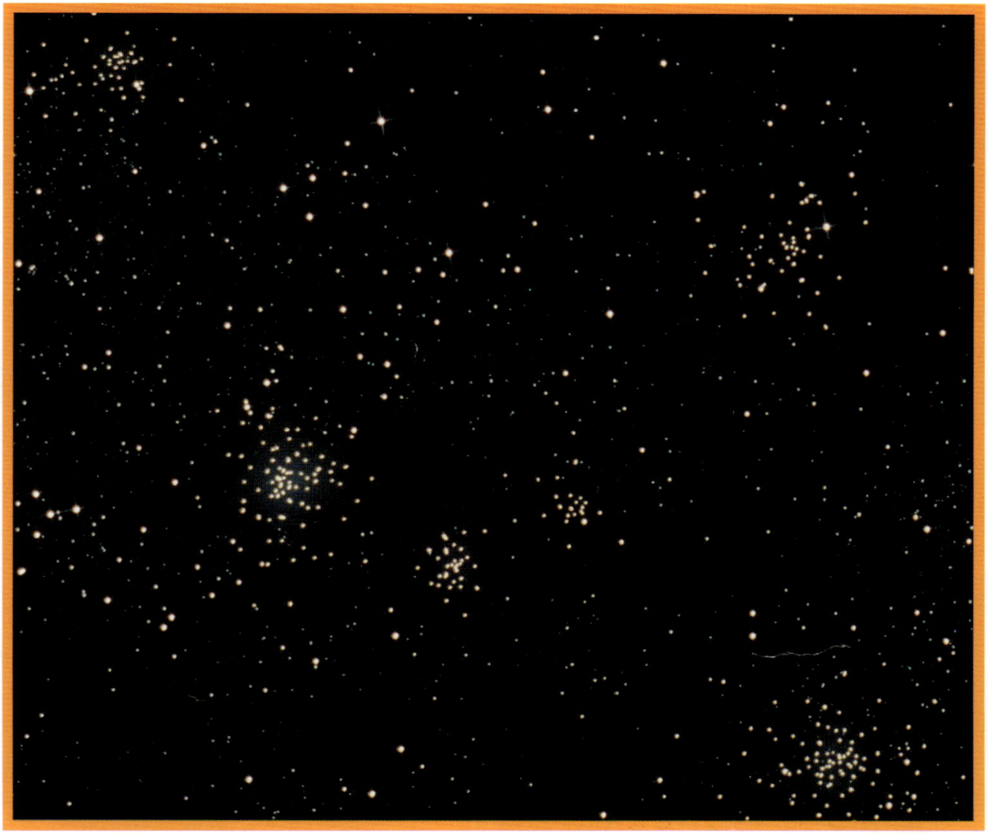

The Sun is a star. It is the closest star to Earth.

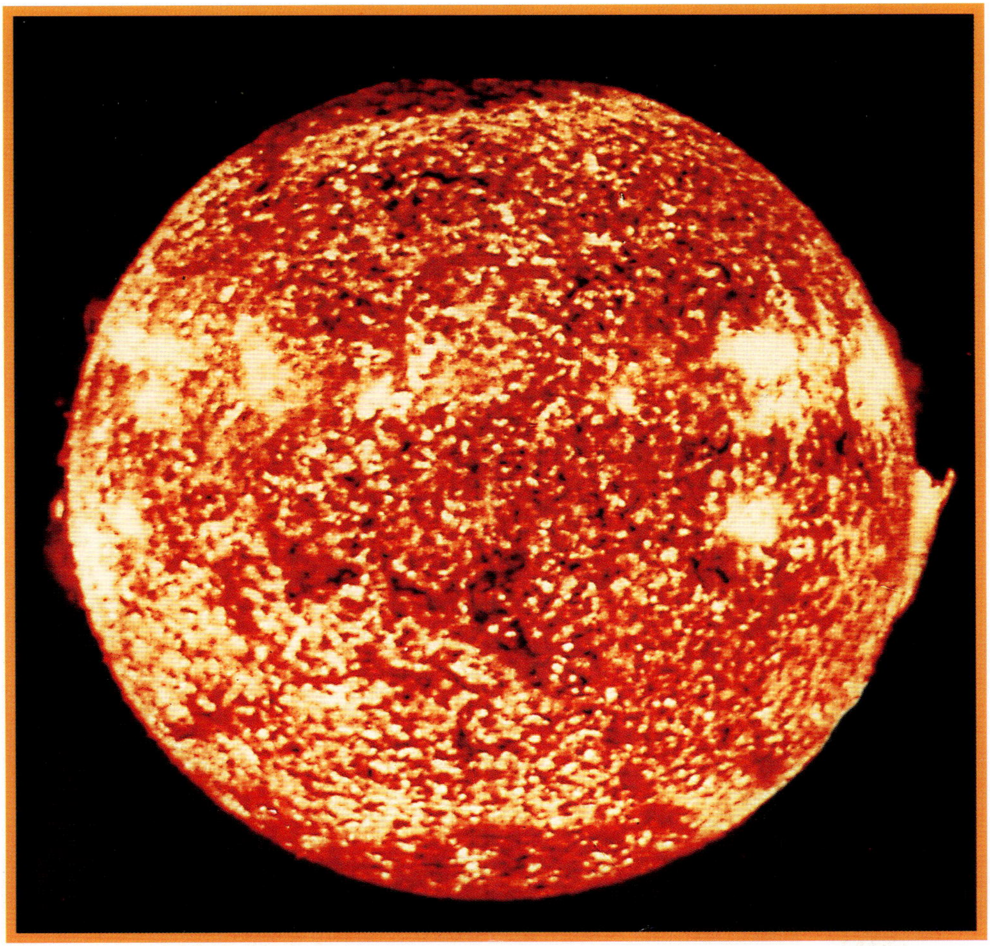

Star patterns

Groups of stars make patterns in the sky. Some of these patterns are called constellations.

This constellation is called Taurus the bull.

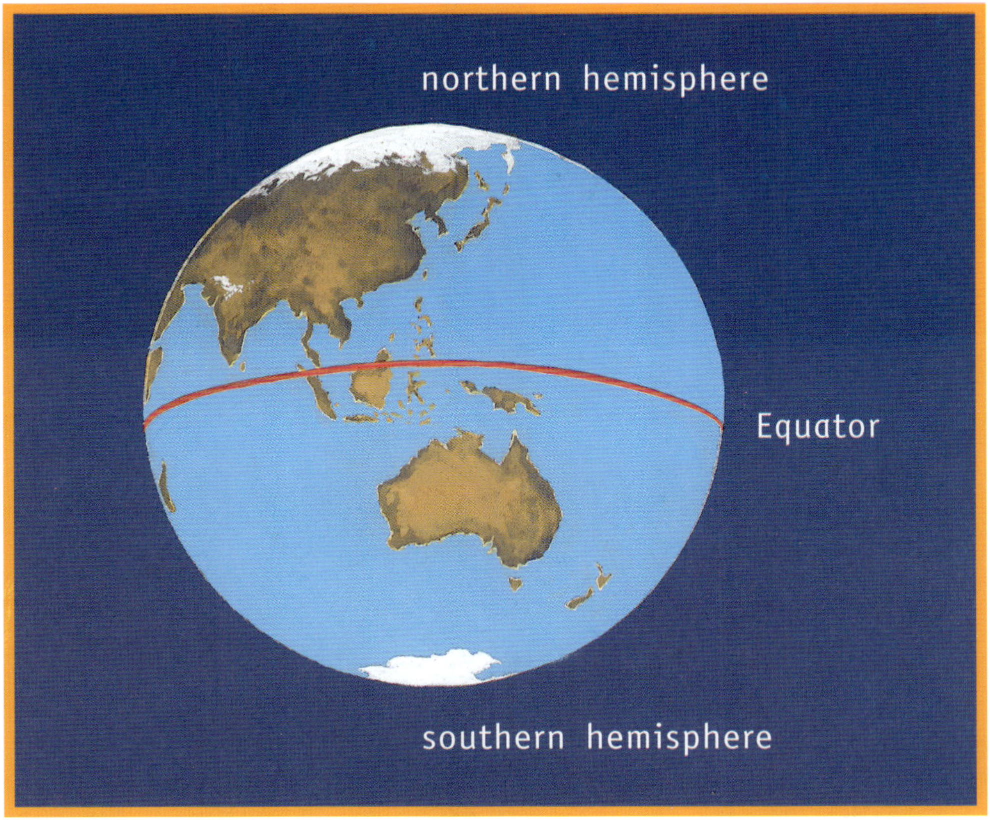

The Earth is divided by an imaginary line, called the Equator, into a northern **hemisphere** and a southern hemisphere. We get a different view of star patterns from each hemisphere.

Orion

Orion the hunter is a bright constellation. The brightest stars of this constellation are Orion's shoulders, belt, sword and legs. This is what he looks like from the northern hemisphere.

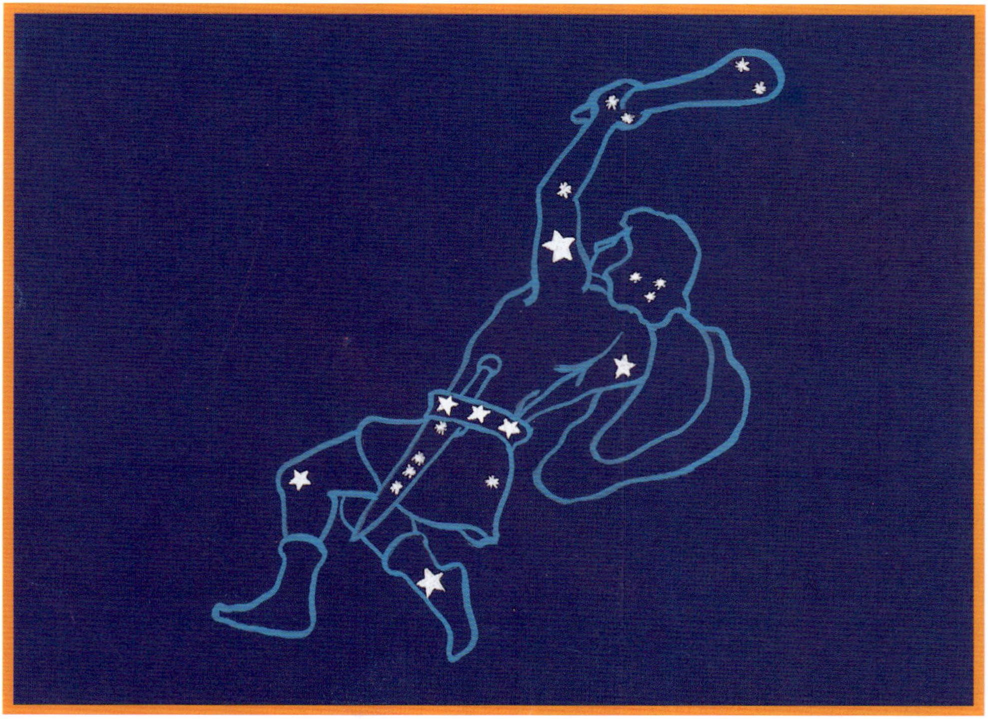

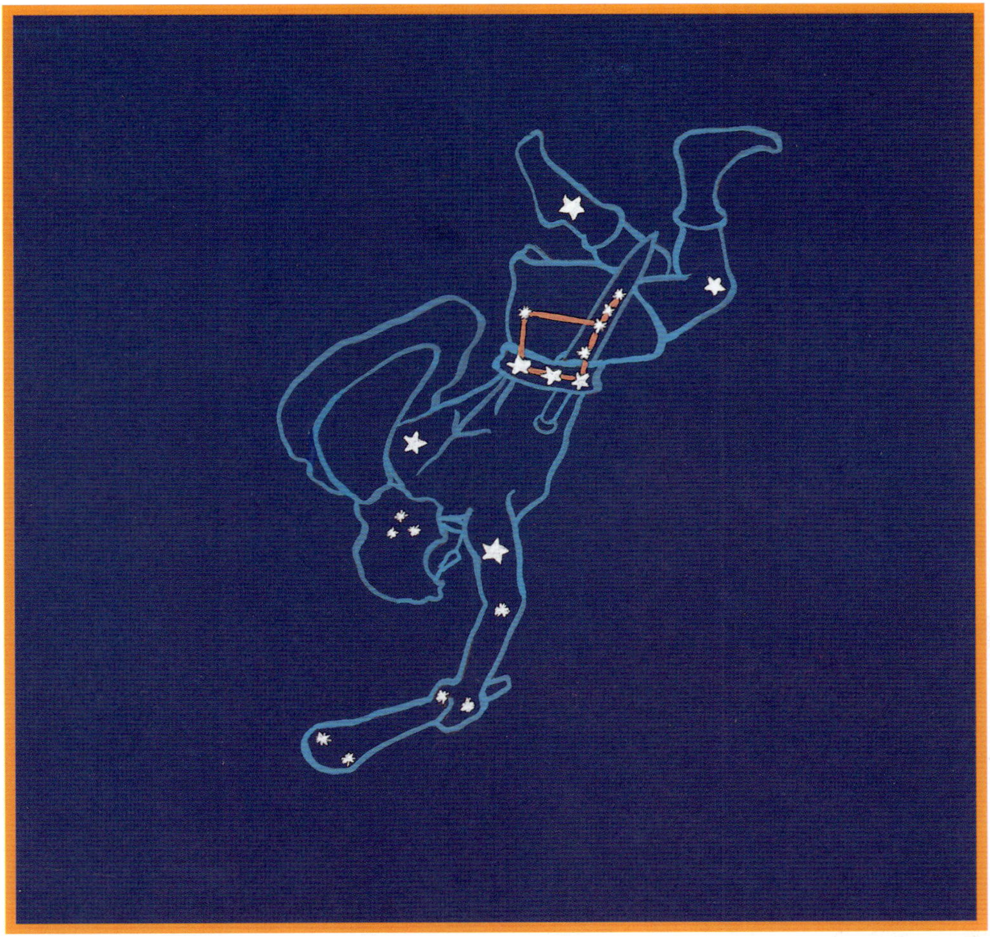

To people in the southern hemisphere, Orion looks upside-down. His belt and sword look like a saucepan.

The Big Bear

The Big Bear can be seen in the northern hemisphere. Its bright stars are also called the Plough or the Big Dipper.

The Southern Cross

The Southern Cross can be seen in the southern hemisphere. There are two stars pointing to it called the Pointers.

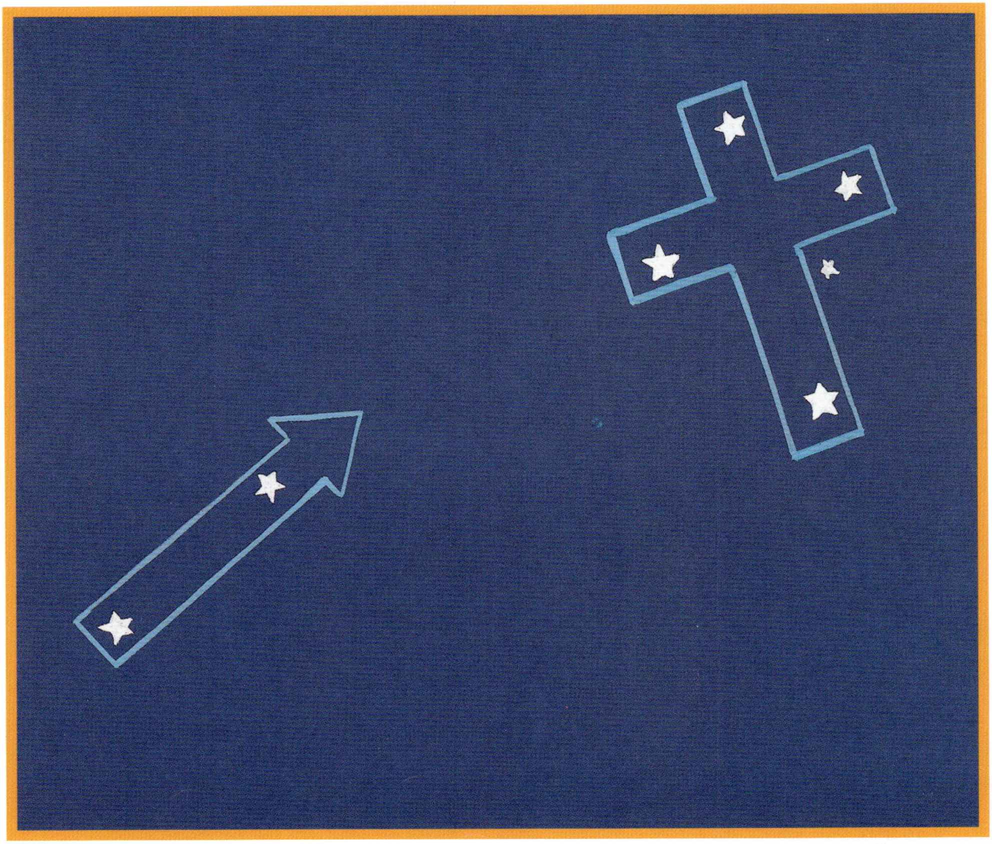

The Big Dog

The Big Dog is Orion's hunting dog. It has a head, back, legs and a tail. It can be seen from almost anywhere in the world.

Sirius

Sirius is the brightest star in the night sky. It is bright white. It is the nose or the neck of the Big Dog.

Scorpius

Scorpius is a huge **scorpion** in the sky. It has claws, a body, and a long curved tail. It has a red star in its body, which is its heart.

Scorpius is on the opposite side of the sky from Orion. In stories, Scorpius killed Orion in a fight. He was sent to the other side of the sky as punishment.

The zodiac

The **zodiac** is made up of 12 constellations.

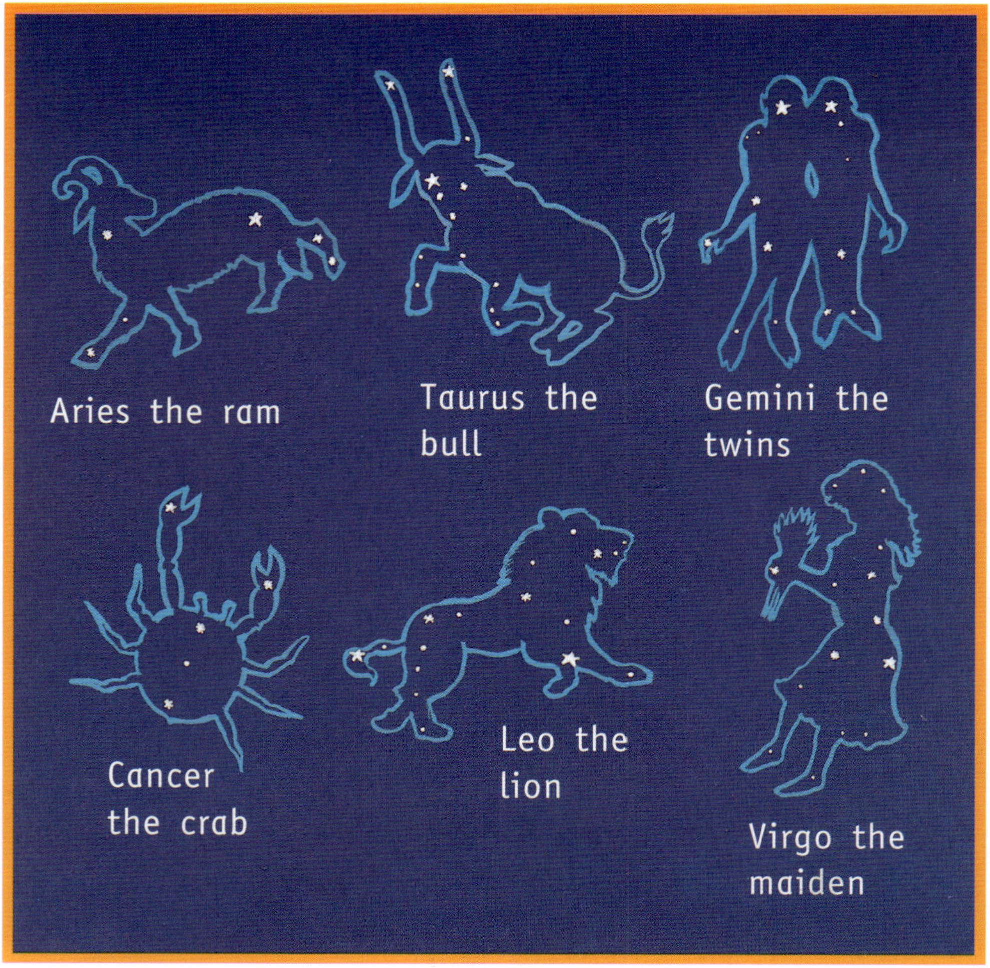

The constellations of the zodiac follow each other across the sky.

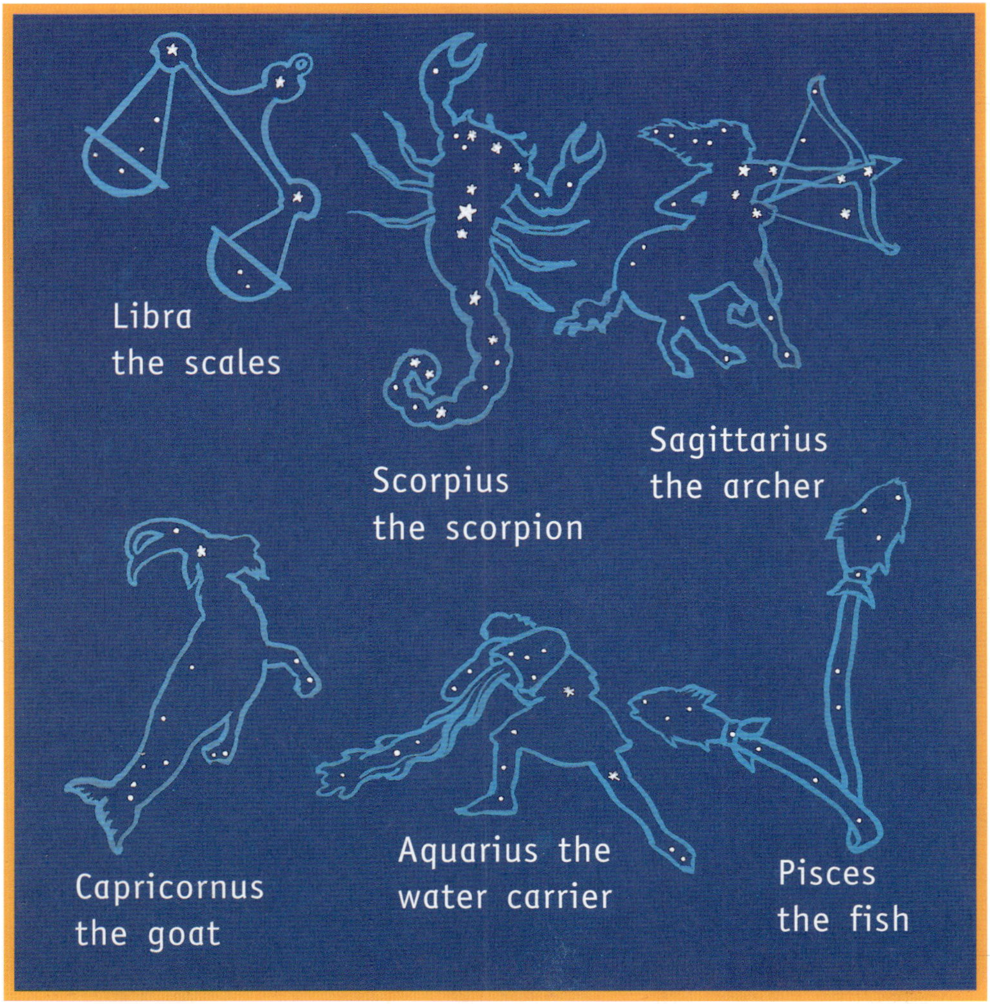

Galaxies

Galaxies are huge groups of millions of stars. The galaxy we live in is called the Milky Way galaxy. It has a **spiral** shape.

The closest large galaxy to our galaxy is the Andromeda galaxy. It is bigger than the Milky Way galaxy. It also has a spiral shape.

The Milky Way

On a very dark night, away from city lights, we can see the Milky Way. It looks like a thin cloud stretching right across the sky. It is really thousands of stars that are very far away.

The Milky Way got its name because people said it looked like milk had been spilt across the sky.

Star clusters

Some stars are in small groups in the sky. They are called star clusters. The cluster called the Jewel Box is near the Southern Cross.

The star cluster called the Seven Sisters has seven bright stars, and many fainter stars. It is part of the constellation Taurus the bull. It makes the bull's shoulder.

New stars and old stars

Clouds of gas float in space. They are the places where stars are born. Often they contain many young stars.

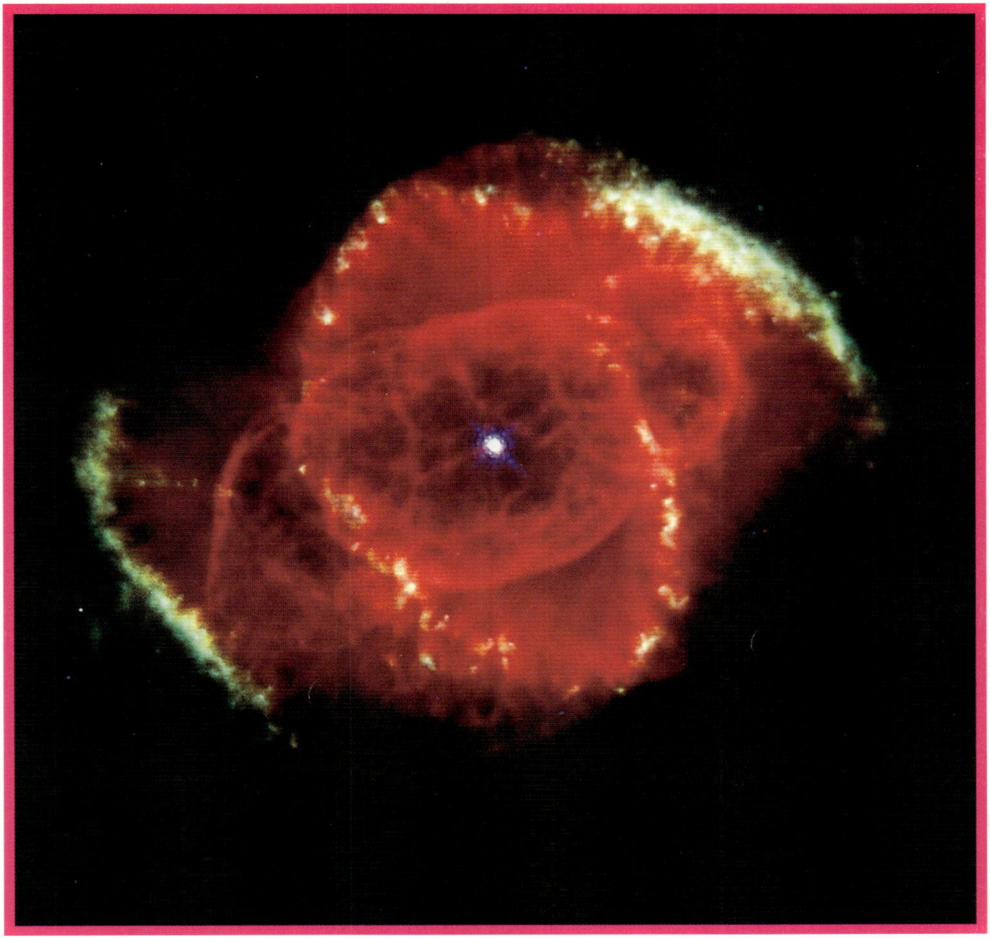

Some stars **explode** when they die. Others die more slowly, and throw off gas into the space around them.

Looking at the stars

The easiest way to have a good look at stars in the night sky is with **binoculars**. They make everything look bigger and closer.

Telescopes also make everything look bigger and closer. They usually make things look upside-down. It is dangerous to look at the Sun with binoculars or a telescope.

Observatories

Places called observatories have very large telescopes. Observatories are often on mountains. They are usually in places where there is no light from cities and towns.

Very large telescopes can show us things that are a very long way away in space. They help us learn more about space.

Constellation facts

Many constellations have scientific names that come from the Greek and Latin languages.

Common name	Scientific name
The Big Dog	Canis Major
The Small Dog	Canis Minor
The Southern Cross	Crux
The Hunter	Orion
The Scorpion	Scorpius
The Bull	Taurus
The Big Bear	Ursa Major
The Small Bear	Ursa Minor

Glossary

binoculars instruments for making things look bigger and closer

explode burst

gas a thin, light substance, such as air

hemisphere one half of the Earth

scorpion a small stinging creature, related to a spider

spiral a coil shape

telescopes instruments for making things look bigger and closer

zodiac 12 groups of stars, which are in a row across the sky

Index